Chris Brazel

Merthyr T

I Found My unique ME

From Tears to Love, Laughter and Joy

Chris Brazel, Author

The moral rights of the Author have been asserted in accordance with the Copyright, Design and Patents Act, 1988.

All rights reserved. No part of this publication may be reproduced, stored in retrieval system or transmitted in any form or by any means, electronic, mechanical, photocopying, recording or otherwise without the prior permission of the Publisher.

The information in this book is the author's opinion and experiences.

Chris Brazel Enterprises Pty Ltd (Publisher) Chris Brazel, Author or the editor shall not be liable (including liability for negligence) for any loss or damage arising out of the information or your use of this book.

First published in 2022 by Chris Brazel Enterprises Pty Ltd, 5/43 Upper Brookfield Rd., Brookfield.

ISBN - 978-0-9805800-9-9

Special thanks to:

The Editor – Marcelle Charles
Formatting – Mindy Gilling
Cover and Design – Chris Brazel

You can contact the Author by email at chris@chrisbrazel.com.au. If you would like to know more about Chris Brazel's work, check out her website www.chrisbrazel.com.au

To buy further copies of the book please order through website www.chrisbrazel.com.au or email chris@chrisbrazel.

This book is dedicated to my sister Lea and Cathy Hallandal.

Amazing people in my life who always know how to make sure I am on track with life.

Chris Brazel

Chapters

1. Introduction

2. My Story

3. Kick Off to My New Life

4. My Codes

5. Action Day

6. Speak Up

7. Turning Point

8. Designer Extraordinaire

9. Message from Chris Brazel

Introduction

Merthyr T

Introduction

Hi, my name is Merthyr T. Yes, I know. Who gives a child a name like that? Well, it used to be worse. Merthyr T stands for Merthyr Thomas and my surname is Waterhouse. My mum's mind sure was not in the right place when I came along.

My mind has not been great as well, until I met up with Henry C and he taught me how to take red flags and turn them into winners.

Not that I had any red flags. I just had a name that everyone would laugh at and bullied me about. I had a mum who was so sad, a sad and messy house and that is only the beginning.

Life was a little hard. I would get a little sad. In fact sometimes I got really sad, and I just didn't want to leave my room.

You know when you go out nothing is going to go right.

Well, that was in the past – not anymore. I want to tell you the story of my life and how I turned it around, even when I thought it was impossible. I guess that is why I got the T at the end of Merthyr. It is all about the turning point. I got the key turned one day when I had enough and went to find a tree where no one else would be. Where I could be alone with my mind. I had enough of the bullies and the world, even my mum and her sorrows.

I sure found a great looking tree but who was sitting there but this boy with messy orange hair, legs crossed singing out "OM".

I thought that would be right even when a girl has had enough of this world someone is there blocking her.

Anyway, as I arrived, he looked up at me we went eye to eye for a split second. It was as if we both saw into each other's soul. For that one split second the world felt different.

We got talking and he told me about being a member of the CB Club and this super colourful lady called Chris Brazel who teaches you to be the unique person you are meant to be. She teaches you that sometimes you just need to put on a set of Unicorn glasses and see the world and the problem in a different way and look for a different solution.

WOW! That day I had found a true friend and you know, even better still I have found the answers and solutions when I feel sad, or the world is not working the way I want it to be. I have turned my name Merthyr T now into a brand. You might even wear one of my jumpers one day or you might buy one of my cookbooks. Who knows where I may end up!

And even better still, I have ,as young as I am, turned my mum around to a whole new life. She now gets up happy, colourful and has even found a new career working with me. Even one better she has a new man in her life not that she has forgotten dad. He is still up there keeping tabs on us both. She just has a new man to love down here. I am sure dad would approve.

Are you ready for my story?

Merthyr T

My Story

Merthyr T

My Story

My story started just before I was born. My mum and dad were so happy together. They would do everything together. Even though I had not been born you could feel the energy, love and excitement while I was still inside my mum.

Then one day my mum and dad were at a special event. It was a big affair. There were lots of families and lots of children.

Halfway through the afternoon the storm clouds came over and it started to rain. Not only rain but then the thunder and the lightning.

We were just inside the marquee with other families. Then, out of the blue, a balloon blew out of the tent. Then this little boy ran out to grab his balloon. It was then that tragedy struck. My dad was struck by lightning as he ran out and saved the little boy.

They tried hard to revive him, but he passed away.

My mum then turned from happy to sad. All of this happened only 3 weeks before I was born.

So, my last few weeks inside my mum were not great.

Finally, the day came and out I came. I thought, wow, I am out into the world. My mum started to cry and hugged me so tight I felt I would explode.

Everything was great for a few days. Lots of people came to the hospital to visit with lots of gifts. They would look down at me and I would just smile. Then it was the time for my name.

Out of the blue my mum comes up with my name Merthyr Thomas Waterhouse.

You want to know how she got to that name? Well Merthyr was the street which was famous where they met and fell in love. Thomas was my dad's name and of course Waterhouse is our surname.

So, mum in all of her wisdom decided she would put all of that together and I would be Merthyr Thomas Waterhouse. But Thomas was not my middle name. Oh no she wanted me to be called every day of my life "Merthyr Thomas." Luckily one of her sisters convinced her to shorten it to Merthyr T. Love my Aunty Lea.

So, I got stuck with Merthyr T as a name and my mum became sad, angry and crying all the time.

It has been 10 years now and she is still in black, our house is a mess, and she is just never happy.

When I go to school the kids there make fun of my name. They have all these horrible nick names. They tease me about having a boy's name as well as a street name. Then because I often start to cry, even though I try hard not to, they then pick on my surname Waterhouse. They say things like here comes the Waterhouse that is always crying.

It is like I do not have any real identity. I feel hopeless, lonely and if this is how life is going to be, it is not great.

I get up each day and I hope each day will be better, but it is just the same. Mum looks so sad in all the black clothes she wears. You never get a happy smile from her. If that is not enough when I get to school the bigger kids then just pick on me.

That is my life one day after another.

Henry C then just looked at me with a grin. Most people do

not smile at me, but he and his orange messy hair and big white glasses just smiled and then he said. "We can fix this."

I thought to myself, "I think you are only eight Henry C." How is an eight-year-old going to help me fix this mess, and you must realize I am only 10 years old."

He then opened his school bag and passed me these awesome glasses. He said, "Just try these on and close your eyes." I thought, "Glasses are for seeing. What is the point of putting glasses on if you are going to close your eyes?"

I took the glasses from him, held them in my hand then said, "What is the point?"

"The point," Henry C said, "Is at the moment you are looking at life one way. I have learnt through this amazing lady called Chris Brazel who teaches children as well as adults you just need to look at life in a different way. So, put on these groovy glasses, close your eyes and imagine what it is that you want. As you look with your eyes closed, take your mind's eye to your soul, make a wish and start to imagine a different life. What would it look like?"

I adjusted the glasses on my nose, closed my eyes and decided to give it a go.

Sitting with my eyes closed, glasses on, Henry C then talked me through the way this is done. How to get to your soul and find the answers.

He said, "Just take 3 deep breaths in and let them out. Now imagine you are walking along the magic road and the road has a destination and at the end of the road, when you reach your destination, you have what you want.

So, all you have to do is keep imagining you are walking along the road, you are nearly to your destination. What do you want to do and see when you get to the T junction?

On the left you have what you already have and your belief about life. On the right is the new road you can walk."

I decided I was going to take the new road to the right.

He then said, "Take five steps down that road and you will have what you want. Then tell me what you see.

What you see will be what sits in your soul. All we have to do is connect you to your soul then we can make wishes come true."

I took the steps, and I knew what he meant. I could feel myself going down inside me. I was going down to my soul and what I really wanted.

It was then I could see my mum dancing, singing and having fun. She was laughing. In fact, we were laughing together.

I could see my dad up in heaven watching us and giving the thumbs up. I could see, which was really awesome, all these t-shirts, and pictures and colourful clothes. I even saw a cookbook that I had written.

I saw my mum and me actually standing at a stall and we were selling the clothes, cards and a book.

I could see people lining up to buy our products. Then as I looked at one of the t-shirts, I saw the label. The label said, "By Merthyr T." I had my own brand. I could see all the kids who had bullied me actually lining up to buy my shirts.

These glasses were great. Wow! My mind was in such a wonderful place. I was really getting into it when I heard Henry C's voice saying that it was time to come back to the real life and hand over the glasses.

I opened my eyes and handed back the glasses. I told Henry C what I saw and felt. His replied, " Well let's make it happen."

I said, "I don't know if you remember but you are eight, I am ten, I have a sad mum, kids that bully me every day and life is not great. So how on earth is this going to happen?"

That was when he said the magic words, "One step at a time. A few prayers, a bit of cleaning, an oil or two, walking, words and water. A chat with Chris Brazel to work out your codes, I reckon we can do this. How about it? Are you ready to join the CB Club and go for solutions not problems, aim high, climb some mountains and take on the world?"

I looked him in the eye just like when we first met and said, "Bring it on." We did a take five and that was the start of my amazing journey.

It was also the start of our HQ Tree at the back of the school yard. We had our own soul place to go to and sort out life.

Are you ready to kick off to a new and amazing journey? As Henry C and I agree it is going to be us kids in the world today who are going to save our parents and the planet. Never underestimate the power of two, for two can move to three and three can move to millions.

Enjoy my journey and see how easy you can turn your life around. At the same time, you may change someone in your family as well. Just as I did with my mum.

Merthyr T.

Kick Off to My New Life

Merthyr T

Kick Off to My New Life

Just as we were getting into how all this was going to work, the lunchtime bell went, and it was back into the classroom.

Henry C and I made a pact to meet the following day at lunch time at our special tree and start to sort out a plan for the future.

For once, going back into school I felt much better, my mind was not so sad, and I felt a glimmer of hope that there may be light at the end of the tunnel. Interestingly enough the bullies never said another word for the rest of the day. Then when I got out of school and was waiting for mum to pick me up, they actually left me alone again.

WOW! Maybe there is something in the energy Henry C is talking about and is going to teach me.

I remember he said that if I am afraid and sad and look down, then the bullies will know they are winning. He said I have to look forward and not look down. That was my first tip and I do believe it has worked. Well for the first day. Let's see what comes tomorrow.

The other tip Henry C gave me was to work on the words I use. He said words are very important and great words takes you to great places while sad words take you to sad places and negative words take you to where you don't want to go.

So, I was ready to test the word game as he called it to my mum when she picked me up. Henry C had given me two tasks to work on - eyes and words.

Mum pulled up in the car and in I hopped. I looked her in the eye and said, "Mum, I have had the best day ever. I trust you had a great day as well."

She actually smiled back. WOW! "This might just work. Normally I get in and have a whinge about my day. She whinges back we both look sad and so the story goes.

Not today. Mum then turns to me and says, "How come you had such a great day?" I said, "Well I met this cool dude with orange hair and large white glasses. He is only eight, but he knows so much about life."

I told her we were going to have lunch together the following day and work on things. She said, "What sort of things?" Here was the tester. What do I say?

"Ah well he is into this yoga thing where you sit under a tree, and you bring your mind to peace. He is going to teach me a bit of yoga and MINDFIT peace. Apparently, this amazing lady teaches children about MINDFIT. It is really interesting."

Mum said "OK." That was the extent of our conversation. We got home. I did my homework, and she did the cooking. Then the usual TV on and then off to bed. Same old routine.

The only difference tonight as Henry C had suggested before I head to bed, give my mum a huge hug and tell her that tomorrow is going to be a great day.

This I did. Before I would just give a hug but a basic hug, we would both look at each other and say good night as if well I guess tomorrow will be same old same old.

Not tonight. Life for me was going to change. I was also going to try to help change life for my mum. I was going use my tips to help her change and create a new life. We had too many good years ahead of us both.

It is amazing, when you feel you have a plan, how easy it is to fall asleep.

Just before I turned off the lights, I took out my notebook and as Henry C had said, I wrote out the worst things that had happened during the day and the best things that had happened during the day. Then at the bottom of the list I wrote out, "Tomorrow is going to be amazing."

Henry C said that if you plan ahead to what you want, chances are it can come true.

So, I wrote my list. I wrote out the last sentence then even though he didn't tell me I put a little love heart and a tick. I now had a future.

I was so excited to get to school the following day. I saw Henry C as soon as I arrived, and we had a quick hello.

He reminded me to stay focussed, not to look down and keep positive. I did all he said and wow I got through to lunchtime with not a word from the bullies. I could not believe it. But as Henry C said, when you get positive and confident and know where you are going often the bullies are not sure what is happening so leave you alone for the time being.

As soon as lunchtime came, I met up with Henry C at our special tree. This was now going to be our HQ to plan out our lives.

He said he has spoken with his mum and that she was going to organise a coding session to work out my codes so we could sort out my mind and what to do.

I said, "But what will it cost? I don't know if I can afford it." He said, his mum was going to check. Sometimes Chris Brazel has these special deals when it comes to helping kids who need a little help.

Then I realised we could use my savings. I had a whole $150 saved up for our holidays. Henry C then said he had a few Pokémon cards that were top of the list that he would trade for me. I said, "Oh no you cannot do that, they are precious to you."

He then turned to me and as usual with his eyes, wide smile, out came the words of wisdom, "A Pokémon card is just a card, whereas you are a person in need. Let's see what mum finds out."

The rest of the day went great. Again, when mum picked me up, I got in with smiles and great words. Again, my smile and great words made her smile, and she even had a laugh about an incident at work.

We then got home and our usual routine. Except now I had an extra routine with my book before I went to sleep.

If my days can be anything like the last two just because of where my eyes went and the words, there is no way I am missing out on this small task.

I arrived at school and sure enough Henry C comes running over. He said that he had great news. His mum spoke with Chris Brazel and explained about me, my mum and dad and here is the deal.

"The cost of the codes will be 10% of your savings which will only be $15.00, and I hand in my Pokémon cards, but they are only as a deposit. She wants to move me up to leadership. So, if I keep focused and help you with these few issues, I get the cards back and my level one badge as a team leader.

I think we have hit the jack pot. Now here is what I need - your date of birth, your house number, your full name, your mums mobile number and your mum's date of birth.

Chris Brazel is going to do all the codes and give them to my mum with a list for us to do. She also agreed to meet with us by zoom if we need any extra help. She said it will be awesome to have more children as leaders and help her grow the CB club.

Even better still, as of this very moment you and I are now members of the CB Club which is worldwide. How cool is all of this? We are official club members."

I was so excited. "Thank you Henry C I don't know how to repay you. See you at lunchtime."

Lunchtime came and again we met under the HQ tree. I went through all the information he needed.

My life was changing. I could feel it in my bones.

For three days now I had not been bullied. I had not needed to cry. Even my mum was starting to smile and guess what, this morning she put on a colourful scarf that looked so nice around her neck.

I know I can make changes in my life and my mum's life especially with the help of Henry C.

Special people always come into your life when you really, really need them.

Merthyr T

My Codes

Merthyr T

My Codes

I got up so excited. I could not wait to get to school and see Henry C and find out about my brain, my codes and me.

Mum beat me downstairs this morning. For the first time in a long time she had the music on in the kitchen.

WOW! Could this be how easy it is to create change in people? She had another colourful scarf on and this time the colourful earrings to match.

I walked up to her and said, "Mum you look amazing, so beautiful." She smiled back and said, "I woke up this morning and just felt different. It must be all those wonderful hugs you have been giving me and those great words you keep using".

It was amazing. We got into the car and for some reason mum turned to me and said ,"How about we take a different route to school this morning? I think we need a little change in our lives." Up went the car radio and off to school we went.

It was awesome. Henry C was right. When you get positive people around you then you get positive.

When you look for answers then people also look for answers. When you speak great words, it rubs off.

I arrived in the playground and sure enough Henry C was there waving his arms up in the air with a grin on his face.

I knew he had my codes. He quickly said, "Catch you at lunchtime, we have a plan to put into place".

The morning seemed to go so slowly, but I think it was because I wanted it to go fast.

I raced to our HQ tree at lunchtime ready to get my codes. I was so excited.

As soon as I saw Henry C he was smiling. He said, "Sit down, you have great codes, there is nothing to worry about."

"Oh, that is great. So, what are my codes?" I said.

"Well, you have an 8, 5, 6, 3,1. All powerful so you are a real winner. Here is a plan of action.

With your 1 code we need to work on your bedroom. The best colours for your bedroom will be fuchsia pink with a touch of red and white.

With the 8 we need to make sure your bed is in the control position. You are an achiever, so we need to make sure you see what you have achieved."

Just then I had to butt in. "Ah, Henry that may be a problem. I don't think I have achieved anything. Not in sport, not in art, I can't think of a single thing. What are we going to do?"

"Merthyr T what have you just done?" "I don't know Henry C."

"You went to the problem. We need to look for the solution."

"Ok I said. Keep going."

"You are very visual, so we need to make sure what you see is what you want to invite into your life.

The reason the bullies are getting to you is that with the 6 code, you can be fearful. That combined with the 8 code means when you don't feel you are in control, they put the fear into you.

Chris Brazel has given me a plan to work with, and guess what, I was so right with the eyes, I just knew it. With your 1/8 codes, where you place your eyes kicks off your power.

The 8 code is karmic – what you give out is what you get back. So, when you were putting your eyes to the ground and not looking up, you were in the past where they had bullied you before, so you were expecting it again. Now you are looking at the present and in the now. You are giving off a whole different energy. I don't think those bullies know what to do.

Now another room in the home is the lounge room so we will have to work on that.

I have to give you the best news of all. You have one of the luckiest codes a person can have with the 3 code. We get you into the right lane to where you want to go, Bobs your uncle and you will be a winner.

This is our list.

- Check out the bedroom.
- Bed in the control position
- Check the curtains
- Check what you see when you look out the window
- Check the pictures on the walls
- Check to see what you see each day when you wake up
- What are the colours in your bedroom?
- How do you put your shoes away?
- We have to keep writing out each day just as I showed you
- We need to work out what you would like to do when you are older
- You need to open up your voice, so you need to kick off a little singing
- You will need to do the ball exercises like me to push through
- Here is the best one. Chris Brazel said that you are very creative,

talented and that you should love being in the kitchen and that one day you could write your own cookbook with original recipes.
- She also said that with your codes you could be a famous designer. It is just up to you what you would love to be."

Just then a little tear came to my eyes. Someone whom I have never met actually knows me without my saying a word.

I was never game to say that I wanted to be famous one day, to be a designer or even write a cookbook. I thought people would think I was stupid.

I then asked how she knew about wanting to be famous, either as a Master Chef or a Clothes Designer. Henry C then said, "It is in your codes. With your 5 code it connects to the kitchen. That should be where your mind comes to peace, and you feel at home."

I then said, "I do." I then asked, "But how did she know I wanted to write a cookbook?"

"Oh, that is your combination of 1 being innovative, 2 being a writer and eight says that you want to aim high and achieve recognition," replied Henry C.

Just then I felt like I could just hug Henry C – this boy was going to save my life.

I must say a few more tears came to my eyes. Henry C just smiled and said, "We are going to make this happen. You are going to get a new life; your mum is going to get a new life and for me, well, I am moving into leadership. We are all going to win."

The bell rang and it was time to go back into the classroom. As we were heading back Henry C said, "Ask your mum if I can come over and have a play date." "Sure," I replied, "Let's do it this weekend."

"Great," Henry C replied.

We were two kids on a mission. No more being at crossroads, being bullied or standing at a T junction not knowing which way to go.

Merthyr T.

Action Day

Merthyr T

Action Day

I was so excited. I got up early. It was Saturday when I normally have a sleep in but not today. Henry C was on the way over and we were on a mission to create a new life for me and my mum.

As Henry C once said, "It may be us kids who actually fix the adults and the planet."

I asked mum if I could do a little baking in the kitchen before Henry C arrived. I wanted to be able to do something special for him for helping me so much. I decided to make my new peppermint slice. I started to research different oils and I found out that peppermint is great for the mind to get it moving with new ideas. From what I have read, when you feel stuck, work with a little peppermint. So, a few peppermint slices should go down well with a glass of mike or orange juice for our meal break.

I could hear a car pull up outside so rushed to the door and sure enough Henry C had arrived with his mum. His mum looked so lovely with her beautiful bright coloured jumper. I thought that is exactly the type of jumper I want to create one day.

My mum and Henry C's mum chatted. We said goodbye and headed towards my room. We had work today.

Just before we were to climb the stairs to my room Henry looked into the living room. He then looked at me. He didn't need to say a word. I just knew so I spoke first.

"I know it is a mess. I know it is sad. I don't think we could fit any more grey or black in it if we tried. Yes, I also know that the cushions are sad with those sad designer pictures."

Henry C just smile, "Never mind. Let's start with your room and we can do this one room at a time."

I had closed the door before I headed down to greet him, as I wanted to give the whole story and the full impression on what needed to be fixed.

I said, "Are you ready?" He smiled and said, "Absolutely, let's do it."

We both stood at the door looking in. I could see his eyes going in all directions. Then he pulled out of his bag the list of what we needed to do and work through.

First – We need to check the bed position.

Not good, you are in the fear position, so we need to move the bed to the control position.

I then said, "Do you think we are strong enough?"

Henry C just replied, "Where there is a will, there is always a way. You don't know if you don't try."

I then said, "Well before we start trying to move the bed, exactly where is the control position?" He then walked over to the wall and said, "This is it. Come and stand here and see how much better it feels."

I walked over and he was right. It felt powerful. I could see the door and out the window. It felt amazing. So much lighter.

We moved the boxes of shoes and the chest of drawers out of the way. I then realised it needed to be cleaned so went and got the vacuum cleaner. Just then mum saw me and asked what was happening.

I said, "Henry C is teaching me how to create great rooms and he is part of the CB Club where you learn how your bedroom affects your mind and it can make you feel sad. I hope that is ok. I just asked him for a little help. I was going to tell you, but I was not sure if you would understand."

My mum then just looked at me with a sad smile. It was like she was happy and sad at the same time. She then said, "Go ahead and if you need any help just let me know."

I said, "Thanks Mum, that is great." WOW! I was wondering how I was going to explain everything.

I took the vacuum cleaner back into the room and started to vacuum where we were going to place the bed.

Henry C then pulled out a spray bottle. I asked, "What is that?" He said, "It is bergamot. Great for releasing. Chris Brazel suggested that as we make changes in the room, we spray a little to give the room a lift and release at the same time."

"Great," I said, "It smells awesome."

We then, with a lot of effort, moved the bed from the fear position to the control position.

Tick – One job completed.

As we stood where the bed was now positioned, I totally understood the difference in how the mind can feel. Amazing when you simply change a piece of furniture that it can change a feeling in your mind and your soul.

"Next," I said.

"Well, your quilt is not great, but we can work on that. What colour are your sheets?" replied Henry C.

"I have grey on at the moment." I said.

"Not good," said Henry C. "Do you have any other colours?"

"I think there may be a pale pink do you want me to go and check?" I said.

"Yes, please," said Henry C. "You are definitely not going to stay in any grey areas of your life.

Sheets are important for that is where you place your body each night to recover from the day and to be ready for the next day."

I was off to the linen cupboard and back I came with pale pink sheets and pale pink pillowcases. On they went.

Each time we made a change I could feel the change within me at the same time. It was like a sigh of relief.

"Next," I said.

"The cupboard with your clothes and shoes," replied Henry C.

I opened the doors and not great. I had tossed all my shoes in the bottom of the cupboard. Things were half on hangers and half off. Nothing was in any sort of arrangement.

I then asked Henry C, "Do you know what cupboards mean with energy codes?"

"Yes," he replied. "I learnt that one early. The cupboard is like what you stuff inside your head in your life. So, the more you feel sad, unsure or lost, the worse your cupboard will be."

Your shoes represent where you are walking to for the future so when you just toss your shoes into the cupboard, it means you don't care about life.

"Well, I am definitely going to care about my life in the future. Show me what I need to do," I said.

"Ok," said Henry C. "Seeing you don't have a 2 and only one 6 code we can give it a good clean out. Chris Brazel said some people cannot handle too much energy change too quickly. They can go into a panic attack. But I checked and we can do as much as you want to, so I suggest we pull everything out. You go through it all and then we only put back what you like and want."

"Great plan," I replied.

Just then mum poked her head around the corner and asked if we were ready for a snack. Even though the room was in a mess she said, "Your room feels better." "Thanks Mum, we are getting there," I said.

Mum left the snack of the peppermint slice and orange juice on the bedside table and Henry C and I took a little break.

This was such cool stuff. We were actually changing my room to change my life. Who knows this could just change my mum as well. Even the small changes I have been making are starting to get her to smile.

We finished the snack and back onto the job. Only what fitted, what I liked and wanted went back in.

My shoes went in all pointing out. Apparently, your shoes need to go together and point out. That way you are setting yourself free without any obstacles in your way. You should try it. Amazing how it feels.

By now we had the bed in the control position.
We now had a clean and tidy cupboard with clothes and shoes. Only the ones that fitted, I liked and wanted.

There was a huge pile of things to go to the Op Shop to help others.

On the bookcase Henry C taught me to stand all my books up. When books are lying sideways that means you are not using your knowledge.

We then tidied up my desk. We moved it so I could see outside the window. I had my back to the door which is not great, but we put the dressing mirror next to it so I could see what was going on behind my back.

We stood back very proud of ourselves. My room looked amazing. It felt amazing.

Then Henry C said, "We just need an inspiring piece of artwork on the wall. I then said, "Why don't I paint my own artwork. That way I will be kicking off my designs at the same time."

"Great idea," said Henry C.

Just then mum walked in. She just stood there. She never spoke and she never moved a muscle. Then I saw a tear come to her eyes. She was happy pleased. That is when you are happy, sad and pleased all at the same time.

She wiped her eye then said, "WOW! you two. What an amazing job. I can't believe how different it feels. I think you have inspired me to do my room."

Just then the doorbell rang, and it was Henry C's mum at the door.

"I better go," said Henry C. I walked over and just gave him a huge hug and said, "Thank You."

"That's ok," he replied. "We are mates and part of the CB club. This is just the beginning of a great journey."

I waved goodbye and headed back up to my room. I could not wait to sleep there that night.

As I completed my writing task for the day, I said a prayer and a thank you to my dad. I kinda thought, I bet you dad you were behind us today and helped move what we needed to move especially the bed.

Love you dad, love you mum, love you world.

Merthyr T

Speak Up

Merthyr T

Speak Up

Well two weeks had passed. My room was feeling great. Mum was actually smiling more, and she had even started to wear coloured accessories each day.

My life, I thought, was WOW and amazing. Then lunchtime came. Henry C was away this day, so I decided to spend my time in the playground. Not a great idea.

Within no time the bully of all bullies with her team of girl followers bowls up as I am eating my lunch and demanded that I hand it over.

I said, "If I give it to you, then I won't have any lunch." Her answer, "So, do I care? AH that would be a big NO. Hand it over or else."

I thought for a moment and a tear came to my eyes. Just when I thought I was progressing to a whole new life, the bullies were back. I decided it was easier to just hand my lunch over. We were sitting near the rubbish bin. As soon as I gave her my lunch in my lunch box, she tossed it into the bin. She then turned to me and said, "Go on Waterhouse, turn on the water works. We just want to let you know who controls this area, and it sure is not you. Be ready for the works, Waterhouse. Every day this week you will be handing over your lunch to us. Don't think you can do anything about it. There is nowhere for you to hide. Got it?"

"Yes," I replied, "I have got it."

Just then the saver, the bell went, and it was time to go back into class.

The rest of the day was not great. I wished that Henry C was here, but he was not. I had tried to look straight and not down, but my mind was in such a state it was too hard.

I also tried not to cry. As soon as the tears would come, I would wipe them quickly so nobody would see.

The day ended and it was time to go home. Mum was on time. I thought, do I tell her or not? As I opened the door I could see by her face and her eyes which were puffed that her day had also not been great. So, I just hopped in, put my seat belt on and we headed home silently, not saying a word. Must check what the moon phase is, as today was not great for us both.

I went to my room and started to write out in my journal. Chris Brazel had put in my codes that I needed to write out the day's problems and release them. Luckily Henry C had left the bergamot oil, so I gave my room a spray. I then wrote out my affirmation to create my powerful mind.

So, interestingly I was actually starting to feel a little better. I then remembered the ball exercise, so I went out the back to the wall and worked with my orange ball and used the words and ball to release the problems of the day. I worked for about half an hour. My mind was feeling much better. By the end I remembered something that Henry C had said.

Nobody has power over you. When someone starts to take your power away you make a choice to get it back. But get it back the right way as everything in life is karmic. What you give out is what you get back.

Night came and bedtime. I said a little prayer to my dad to see if he could help from above.

Morning came and I was ready. No bully was ever going to rule me and my life again. Besides she is only 11. Who gives her the right to my life?

I didn't say anything to my mum. She had enough on her plate, I had Henry C by my side who will know the answers.

Phew, he was right at the gate waiting for me. It was like he had sensed that I needed his expertise.

I walked up to him and told him what had happened. Just then I could see out of the corner of my eye the 11-year-old bully with her bully followers. Henry C turned to see what I was looking at. He asked if that was the one who had threatened me.

I replied "Yes." He then said, "Right, this ends today. You and I are off to the Principal's office."

I said, "Henry C are you sure? What will the bullies do to me?"

Henry C said, " If we don't speak up today, they will just get worse. You don't want to change schools, do you?" "No," I replied.

"Well let's go," said Henry C, so off we went to the Principal's office.

We arrived. I had Henry C by myside. Luckily, we were able to see the Principal immediately. I explained to her what had happened the previous day.

It was so nice that she believed me. She then said, "Right, at morning tea and lunchtime, come immediately to my office and you and your buddy will eat here.

I will ring the girl's mum and your mum and ask that both mothers meet me today in this office. We will be working on this immediately.

Bullying is not accepted in this school.

She then turned to us both and asked, "Do we have a plan?" "Yes," we replied.

Then off we went to the classroom and the day went fine with our plan.

Mum turned up and knew that we had to go to the Principal's office. We sat there with the bully and her mum.

The bully just kept giving me weird looks. I just looked her back directly eye to eye.

The meeting went great. I told the whole story. The bully could not deny anything.

The Principal then told the bully she would be spending every morning tea break and lunchbreak in detention. She made it very clear that bullying would not be tolerated in this school.

The bully's mum accepted the punishment and said she would be working with the problem with her daughter at home.

Phew, it was over. I spoke up. I was believed. Action was taken.

My life was now going to get on this new amazing track that Henry C had been helping me with.

Mum and I headed home and mum made sure that I knew that if anything of this kind happened again, she wanted to know immediately. I agreed.

Mum wanted me to know that no matter how bad her day went, she was still there for me and whatever was troubling me. I said, "Thanks Mum, I love you." She replied, "I love you too."

I never had a problem with that bully or her friends again. She got the message. Mess with me and I will be reporting you to the Principal.

Trust me. If you are reading this book, tell the truth and speak the truth and people will believe you.

Never accept a bully in your life. Speak to your mum or dad, brother, sister or teacher. Everyone is here to help you.

The truth always finds solutions.

Now let's get to the happy journey of my life. Enough of the sad days. Trust me that from this occasion forward, mum and I moved into the magic of life. We were totally brand new, on a mission to have the best life we could.

Merthyr T

The Turning Point

Merthyr T

The Turning Point

It has been a few weeks now since Henry C and I have been working together.

He is amazing and even though we are at different ages, we get along super. It is awesome.

We have had a few sad chapters up to now talking about my life, but from now on I promise you it is going to be an exciting journey with me.

It was Wednesday. I think one of the best days in my life.

I was up early and ready to go to school. Mum was in the kitchen waiting for me for breakfast. WOW! She looked so different. She had a bright coloured top on, bright earrings even lipstick.

I said, "Mum you look amazing. What is happening?" She then explained that she had called Henry C's mum and asked if she could catch up for a coffee and find out more about Chris Brazel and her work. So apparently all this happened on Monday. My mum and Henry C's mum had a coffee and a zoom meeting with Chris Brazel.

Mum got her codes done and so started to totally understand why her mind was thinking the way it was. Also, why she had the house in a mess the way she did. Why she was still in the past with so many things. Apparently, she has an 18 energy that can connect to a past event that is hard to move on from.

Mum was so excited telling me about her meeting with Chris Brazel and Henry's C mum. She was even more excited for as soon as she drops me off to school, Henry C's mum and her were going shopping. Then Henry C's mum was coming back to the house, and they were going to totally feng shui the house and give it all new energy, changing pictures, cushions even bed linen on both her and my bed.

Mum said, "Merthyr T, when you come home this afternoon you are going to enter into a whole new world of happy colours, pictures and the new arrangement of furniture. I have organised for Sam's mum to pick up both you and Henry C and come back for a celebration and grand opening of our new home environment. I learnt so much on Monday working with Chris Brazel about how our home affects our minds in so many ways."

I walked over and gave mum the biggest hug I could. We were then off to school. I was so excited I could not wait to chat with Henry C.

The day went really quickly, and Sam's mum was there to pick all three of us up.

Even Sam's mum was excited to see the new place. Even more amazing Sam's mum was in a bright coloured top, bright coloured earrings and super fab shoes.

We arrived home, flew out from the car ready to open the door.

Just as we arrived at the door the music started from inside. It was one of my favourite songs, "We will Rock You."

Mum opened the door, her energy super high. She was happy, she was smiling and she was loving in so many ways.

Next Henry C's mum came to the door. All three mums started to hug each other.

Us kids walked in to see what had been happening. The house for a start smelt fab. It was like an orange sweet smell.

First room the lounge room. Spotless. No mess on the floor. No items all over the couches.

There was a new piece of artwork on the wall. I recognised it from the Chris Brazel collection, "Sunflowers." Then the cushions on the couch matched the picture.

The room just look so beautiful and happy. No more black on grey with sad pictures. This room had spark.

Next was the dining room. No more bills and paperwork all over the table leaving only a small place for us to eat. The table was shining with a large bowl of oranges in the centre.

Next into the kitchen, my favourite room. A picture of mum and me on the fridge with the words, "Awesome times ahead."

A vase of flowers which Henry C's mum had brought over was on the bench.

I turned to mum and said, "Mum this is amazing. Everything looks so different. I then turned to Henry C's mum and said, "How can I thank you for giving back our home and my mum? I can feel our life is going to be so different."

Henry C's mum bent down and gave me a huge hug. Then she said "Merthyr T, you have been the best thing for Henry C. He comes home every day with exciting news. You see he used to always feel alone and different at school, so it works both ways. We all just need to work as a team and help each other out."

Just then mum said, "Go up and check out your new room. Henry C, along with Sam and I, flew up the stairs to my room

I opened the door. I had the most beautiful pink, white and green quilt I have ever seen. Next, I looked on the wall and sure enough I had the Unicorn Horse in the garden. One of my favourite prints by Chris Brazel. I truly felt like a princess.

Next mum sang out from downstairs, "Take a look in my room as well."

We rushed over to see what mum's room looked like. Sure enough, totally changed. It looked calm, peaceful and beautiful.

I then looked to the side wall and there was a picture of mum and dad when mum was pregnant with me. They both looked so happy. It totally finished off the room.

After checking everything out, the boys and I headed downstairs for our afternoon celebration.

Three families all sharing great times.

Henry C, Sam and their mums left after our celebrations, and it was just mum and I.

Mum turned to me and said, "How about we go for a little walk and start planning our future. I learnt from the zoom lessons with Chris Brazel that walking is excellent for both of us so I think we will put a walking schedule in each week. Chris Brazel also mentioned that you and I both have designer codes. I was thinking, I know you love cooking, and you can always do that, but how would you like it if we kicked off a t-shirt, sweater and special items design business? Something the two of us could do together."

I turned to mum and said, "Unreal, do you mean it?"

"Absolutely," was her reply. You can design and I can put the graphics to the designs, then we can build our business for the future."

I then looked up to the sky and with a smile and a squeeze of my mum's hand said, "Thank you Dad, I may not have met you in person but with you upstairs, you are with me every day in every way."

Mum smiled at me, and we continued our walk chatting about all the types of designs we could do.

The Turning Point had come for both of us in more ways than just one.

No matter where you are today, please always know that you can be somewhere different tomorrow. In fact, you can take your mind to somewhere different right this minute.

Just stop for a minute and allow your imagination to go to where you want it to go.

It is through imagination, thoughts and words then action, that you too can create a turning point in your life and your family's life.

We can change the world, one step at a time, one person at a time, one family at a time.

It all starts with a decision, then little choices lead to big wins.

Merthyr T

Designer Extraordinaire

Merthyr T

Designer Extraordinaire

Once everything settled from our big day of changes in the home, mum and I would sit after dinner and before I went to bed discuss the designs we could do as our business.

As mum said, "You are never too young to kick off a business." She also said that dad was a real entrepreneur and would be so proud of us both using our creative skills in a business to help others be happy.

Mum suggested that we take animals, colour and words and match to inspiring designs to help people be happy. Mum knew I had a real love for animals and their special loving energy.

She had bought the Animal Energy book that Chris Brazel had written so I knew the energy of all the animals and how to match animals to words to colour to create positive minds for people.

There was a creative arts market coming up in a few months so we both decided to get into the designs and have a stall at those special creative arts markets.

Each day when I would get home from school, I would take out my pen and paper and start drawing different animals.

The drawings and designs were ok, but I felt they could be better. I was getting a little worried as the creative arts market day was getting closer and we still did not have any actual designs that we were both happy with.

Then one afternoon when mum and I arrived home, I was about to put my suitcase in the usual place and head for a milk and cookie. Mum said, "Why not head up to your room. I have a little surprise for you up there."

A surprise. What could it be? I opened the door and there sitting on my bed was the cutest sausage dog there could be.

She was standing on my bed wagging her tail. She was a beautiful tan colour. She had a pink collar with little diamond studs. My heart started to pound at a million miles an hour.

The happy feeling inside was out of this world. I rushed over and picked up this beautiful little dog. As soon as I had her in my arms, she started to lick me.

By this time mum had arrived at the door and said, "What do you think?"

I said, "Mum, how can I ever thank you. She is so beautiful. I love her. How did you know I so wanted a little dog?"

"It is all in your codes. When I had my codes done Chris Brazel mentioned that it might be great at one stage for you to have a little puppy as that would help you connect to your inner soul and be able to release the love within. You would be able to share.

So, I thought maybe the little block that is holding us back on our designer business might be that we both don't think we are good enough or deserving or worthy to be great designers.

So, taking on board our mind codes and the advice of Chris Brazel, this is our new member of the family.

You can name her whatever you like."

"Thank you, thank you, thank you. I can't say it enough times." I said.

"I am going to name her "Princess" as she is truly a princess in our lives."

The next day after school I rushed home, opened the door and sure enough there was Princess waiting for me. I headed right into our studio and started to draw.

There was no stopping me now. Within the hour I had the perfect design. It was a design of Olli – Henry C's cat sitting and reading a book. The words that I put with the design were, "Knowledge is the Key". I knew this was something Henry C and Chris Brazel would say all the time.

For when you have knowledge you can make great decisions. Always know your facts and figures. I used Henry C's cat "Ollie" as I wanted to make sure that he received one of my first designs. I also knew that cats relate to self-esteem and self-worth, and this is what I find most people don't have about themselves.

I showed mum my first drawings. She said, "Great, they look awesome. Let's get this show on the road."

We were on our way. The kick off would feature "Ollie" as our starting guest but then I would move to "Princess" and her range. I could see now I could move each month to the different animals.

I had a grand plan in place. I had a great business partner. We were on the road to fame and fortune. Not that these were all we were after. What I simply wanted was to take my creativity and passion for design to the world.

The day of the creative arts market arrived. We were ready. We had lots of t-shirts, sloppy joes and even socks. We also had library bags ready to sell.

The table with our display looked amazing. As soon as we had everything set up, people started to walk over and look at our designs.

Then we had our first sale. Mum let me take the money while she wrapped the sloppy joe.

Our designs were selling like hot cakes. It was so exciting.

Just then I looked up and who was walking towards our stall but the bully from school with her mum.

I thought, " I can either be scared and hide or I can look her in the eye and say hello, which is what I did."

They arrived at the table and both mums said hello. I then looked at the bully and with a smile said, "Hello, you look nice today with that dress and the bow in your hair."

To my surprise she answered back that our table of designs looked awesome and asked would it be ok to buy one.

Well, my heart raced, I was speechless. Then blurting out, I said "Absolutely. Which one do you like the best?"

She actually picked one that I thought was my best design. I said, "Why not try it on, which she did." I then said, "I think that design was made for you especially."

She then turned to her mum to ask if she could buy the sloppy joe.

Just as her mum was about to reply I looked at my mum and I think we both thought the same thing at the same time. I said "I would love to give you this design as a gift, Emily."

WOW! For the first time ever I had used her name. She then said, "Oh no, you don't have to do that." I then said "I know I don't but sometimes it is important that you do things just like this. I would love to wrap it up and it is my gift to you."

Emily smiled back, in fact I am sure there was a little tear in one of her eyes.

I turned to mum and said, "I can wrap this one, I want to put a little extra energy and a spray of perfume to make it very special for her." Mum stepped to the side and started to chat with Emily's mum.

I finished wrapping and walked around from the table so there was nothing between us and handed Emily her designer gift. Emily then said, "May I give you a hug to say thank you."

I said, "Sure." We both then lent forward and gave each other a hug. As we were hugging Emily whispered in my ear, "I am sorry, can you please forgive me for being so nasty to you?"

I whispered back, "Absolutely, let's be friends."

The end of the day finally came. All our designs were sold out. We even had a list of orders to fill.

Mum did the maths and we made $500 for the day. We were on a winner.

Best of all we sang our favourite songs all the way home, and sure enough when we opened the door, there was Princess to greet and love us as well.

I trust you have enjoyed my story and the journey to this point.

This is not the end. In fact it is just the beginning. I hope to see you at one of the CB club meets. Or maybe you can buy more of my books and adventures. You might even buy one of my designs and wear it someday.

Before I go. I wish you well. Always remember life can change for the better. In fact, life can change to be great.

- Always ask for help if you need help.
- Always speak up and don't let people bully you.
- Know that your bedroom totally represents you as well as your home so even a tidy up can help your mind.
- Know that parents can have days that don't always go to plan. Our job is to be understanding and I believe they need our help from time to time to get on track with life.

If you need to know more about the home, colours, crystals and how to get your mind right, join the CB club. It is an awesome club with great people.

This is me out for now – I have lots more designs to do.

Merthyr T

A message direct from Chris Brazel

Thank you for being part of my world.

Always remember where there is a will there is always a way.

If we speak positive words our minds move into feeling so much better.

If we wear colourful clothes, we feel so much happier each day.

Come and join my club. It is fun and I would love for you to come along. You can even bring your dog along if you like.

Chris Brazel

Notes

Chris Brazel Products

Check out our website for artwork, t-shirts, other books.

Join our club or come join a boot camp.

www.chrisbrazel.com.au

www.ingramcontent.com/pod-product-compliance
Lightning Source LLC
Chambersburg PA
CBHW062104290426
44110CB00022B/2713